Happiness

Noah Shelton

"Being happy never goes out of style."

–Lilly Pulitzer

CONTENTS

Introduction

It is in the human nature to look for happiness. Some look for it in money, prestige, drugs or any other stimulants. Sorry to say, none of these things are the answer to constant joy. You may have played by the rules all your life, have a job that you love and gotten married to your dream partner but are you really happy? You may be living your childhood dream; does that automatically mean that you are happy? If living by the rules and achieving goals were the recipe for happiness, then fulfilling the American dream would be the ultimate solution. Unfortunately, it is not. It is then no wonder that Americans spend over 2 billion dollars annually on happiness books and even more on self-help gurus.

People have their own happiness and theories on how to achieve it. The bottom line is; everybody longs to be happy. However, people are too busy looking for happiness that they have forgotten to pause and live in the moment. People overlook the most basic things in life such as smiling, being grateful for what they have, enjoying the sunny day and being kind to others. It is not surprising then to know that over 90 percent of the world population is chronically unhappy.

But what is this "happiness" that you are talking about?

Human beings natural state should be constant peace. However, as you grow older, life's turmoil and ever-changing circumstances either disturb this peace or in some cases bury it. Just like physical objects, when peace stays buried long enough, you forget that it was there to begin with, and this is when the search begins. Just because you forgot you have what it takes to be happy, does not mean you no longer have it. Desire and fear are the roots of unhappiness, when you fulfil a desire or eliminate the causes of fear you tend to be happy for a certain period, no matter how short it may be, you are in absolute peace and true happiness. Unfortunately, life without fear or desires is impractical and even if it were achievable, it would be dreadfully boring. For this reason, you need to master how to control your desires and fears so that they do not agitate the mind and only then will you fully enjoy constant happiness.

To be truly happy begins with understanding what happiness is. The reason why you may be unhappy may be that you have been looking for happiness in all the wrong places. If you are looking anywhere outside your being, you will never find it because your happiness lies within you. Human beings are designed to be happy, but life events agitate the mind therefore disturbing that peace. Consequently, people feel unhappy over time; the peace is long forgotten, and it is as if it was never there to begin with. Happiness is more than pleasure or excitement; it cannot be stimulated by events or circumstances that are imperative for the achievement of constant contentment. It is also paramount to take note that the happiness state is not dependent on what others expect of you; it depends on how much you love yourself and the magnitude of how much you are impressed with whom you are. Some people spend years in school to prove that they are not losers, others marry to prove to their friends, family or even to the world that they are mature, and responsible, yet they are still unhappy. If you do something with the intention of getting approval since you believe it will make you happy, you are as misguided. Whom are you trying to make happy: yourself or others?

Bill Cosby once said that laughter turns even the most painful circumstances around. To be as happy as you can be, you should not bother too much about life's fairness, whether it is or not, learn to flow with it, and to take pleasure in the scenery as well as the detours. So, why are you in this world if not to take a stroll and enjoy its beauty? Replay good thoughts in your mind, and when bad things happen to you, write them on the sand, marble or fine things, you may be surprised at how happy your days might become. Happiness does not mean that everything is perfect; it only means that you have chosen to look beyond the imperfections. You have to avoid all the reasons to be subjected to any form of restriction or obstruction brought about by any setbacks. You have to surround yourself with happy thoughts for happy and beautiful things to happen.

Being able to remain calm and unaffected even in the face of chaos is not a talent; it is an art that can be acquired over time. It takes mindful practice and patience but as soon as you start to enjoy the yields of your hard labour, which is true and constant happiness, your efforts will be well warranted. This book is aimed to prompt you to analyze your life closely enough to find out the roots to your unhappiness. It will help you have a better and deeper understanding of what true happiness is as well as guidelines and tips on how you can achieve and maintain it. In addition, it will help you to find out the wrong perception you may have regarding happiness and unhappiness. Life is a river of time. It keeps flowing no matter what. Every moment is now. Now creates your past. Now affects your future. The things you do, think, and feel right now affects the flow of your life. Live a happy life on purpose.

Chapter 1: What is True Happiness?

This question has agonized many over the centuries. From scientists to religious and social leaders, everyone seems to have their version of what happiness is or should be. It is not possible to be happy when you do not know what happiness is or at least, what it is not. Happiness is neither having everything you want, nor is it a state of feeling good all the time. Happiness is a state of peaceful, calm contentment; it can also be defined as the elimination of any kind of suffering or want.

The oxford dictionary defines it as "a state of being, feeling, or showing pleasure or contentment." However, the best definition is by the Greeks who defined it as a *civic virtue that requires lifetime cultivation*. Today people have changed this definition to mean maximization of happiness and minimization of pain. This is the wrong approach. This is to blame for the ever-rising demand for happiness self-help books and coaches. Being content is far from the state of not looking for anything, which is the definition of a boring life. It only means that you are okay with the way things are. It means that circumstances do not control your feelings.

The things that bring about happiness are the things that may surprisingly not be on your list. Take wealth, for example, money can buy you countless delightful things but a lot of money is not a guaranteed recipe for happiness. Study shows that any income above the one enough to meet your basic needs improves your life but has very little contribution on your life satisfaction hence very little influence on how happy you are. A good education or material possessions will not bring you long-term happiness.

However, there are certain groups of people who are generally happier than others are. For instance, married people seem to be happier than singles and so do older people when compared to the youth. This can probably be explained by the reasoning behind the scientific definition of happiness. Researchers defined happiness as how much you are satisfied with your life. It is experiencing the 'feel good' feeling on a day-to-day basis regardless of the changes in your life. According to science, overall happiness is genetically determined and not dependent on your mood swings or changes in .k5(e)-u As and circumstances. However, more studies have revealed that a concerted effort can help improve happiness for people who do not have ample presence of the 'happy' gene. You can think of being happy as any physical aspect of your body, such as weight. The way you eat exercise and take general care of your body influences your body weight. If you eat more or less, than you are accustomed to or exercise more or less, your weight tends to adjust accordingly. If you stick to your new diet or exercise regime, then you will maintain in this new weight but if you go back to your old eating and exercise habits, your weight will return to where he began. Consequently, you must learn to control your feelings, and with practice, you can form a lifelong habit, more satisfying and fulfilling life ability.

The majority of people confuse happiness for stimulation or excitement. Activities such as taking drugs, going on a roller coaster ride or having sex give you feelings causing excitemu A. There are other forms of mild excitement, such as eating your favorite meal or watching a great movie, which may not cause an adrenaline rush. The end of stimulation is usually the peak of excitement; this is because of the satisfaction that comes with accomplishing something you have been longing for. You may think that if you find the things that make you happy and lock them in, you can sustain that excitement and turn it to happiness. This is unrealistic and impractical because a few minutes or hours after performing an exciting activity, your mind will ask for more. With time, you will realize that the same activity that used to cause your excitement, no longer has that effect. This is the reason behind most people's non-ending search for excitement. Happiness does not mean a few moments of 'high' or present arrangement of situations. Genuine happiness must come from the heart.

True happiness can be realized when you look inward and locate the things that you believe will continuously spark your life. *Impressing others will never make you happy.* Impressing yourself will. So look in the mirror and if you do not like the person staring back at you, know it is about time you made those all-important and very necessary changes and only then you will find happiness.

Happiness is not something that just happens; you have to choose to be happy. Work towards being happy and devote yourself to maintaining the state of being happy. If you find your inner happiness, it will then be transferred to your work, your family and friends, your business and before you know it, your life will be filled with positivity.

Causes of unhappiness

Happiness is a state of mind. This is one statement you have probably heard a thousand times. The big question is not what it is but how to achieve that status. With hundreds of thousands of articles, blogs and books offering information on how to be happy, it is evident that the information on how to become happy is highly sought after. This reflects just how unhappy the modern generation of mankind is. You may have everything in terms of wealth and all the comfort you wish for but still be asking the question "Why am I unhappy?"

You cannot seem to place a figure on the reason for your constant unhappiness. Fear and desire are the root causes of misery. If you reflect on your life, you will notice that either or both of these emotions have a big stake in your unhappiness.

Happiness is more of a personal choice, but most people are still unhappy. This does not mean that everyone who is unhappy wants to remain unhappy, no. Things like bad relationships, job that you are not fond of, indecisiveness and lack of direction are among the things that affect a person's sense of worth and their happiness. Human beings are emotional beings, therefore when things are not right in their lives they tend to get depressed. Bad jobs or poor working conditions make an individual uninspired. When you have to do something against your will, you are most likely to feel frustrated and with time, the stress might take a toll and result to sadness. Ill health and bad body shape is probably one of the most common causes of unhappiness. Bad health may mean that one is in physical pain, or in the case of a condition such as obesity, one could feel emotionally vulnerable. All these factors can bring about negative thoughts and emotions thus making it hard for a person to be happy.

Happy Homework

Grab a notebook and a pen. You are going to write down everything that you are not happy with. To understand yourself and your happiness more it's a good idea to examine it. Think of as many things as you can. Beside each thing you write down decide if it is a fear or a desire.

Chapter 2: Where Does Happiness Come From?

It is fair to say that so many people are wondering how and where to find happiness, and the truth is, most of them do not have even the slightest idea on where to begin the search. The reason why the hunt for happiness is and will always be on everyone's 'to-do' list is that human beings are designed to be happy. Your being will always strive to be in its original state hence you cannot find peace unless you are happy. Happiness comes from within and nothing but yourself can bring you happiness. Learning to appreciate what you have, no matter how much or little it is and by starting from where you are instead of postponing it until 'when' or 'if' something happens.

Happiness comes in three different ways:

The first and the most basic way to be happy is relying on the naturally occurring joy that resides in your core. You are not required to do anything special to create this happiness, but the things you feed your mind on a day-to-day basis often cloud it hence preventing it from flowing naturally. When you abide in your natural state of mind, not anger, fear, excitement or any other emotions can distort that peace. The second source involves training your mind to be peaceful and happy. For example, you may choose to love your thoughts, words and actions. When you cultivate love, joy, justice and compassion, you are bound to become happier. Lastly is the happiness you get from your external environment. Living a dream definitely contributes to how happy an individual will be or at least will not. A great career, a perfect marriage, awesome weather and any other aspect of your life does play a part in your happiness, but that is subjective to the person. However, their contribution is very low to the extent that most people argue that it is negligible.

Your genetic composition also has a lot to do with how happy you are. Scientists believe that human beings have a gene that acts like naturally occurring Prozac. If you have a long version of the gene, you are likely to be naturally happy and if you are among the unlucky ones who were born with a shorter version of it, you are most likely to be generally unhappier compared to the others. In fact, it is estimated that 50 percent of your total happiness is dependent on your genetic composition. Guess that explains why some people look like they wake up on the wrong side of the bed every day. The happy gene is unlocked by acts of kindness and compassion. When you extend an act of kindness to someone, you get the kind of peace and contentment by the mere fact that you helped someone breathe easier. Everyone, regardless of their gender, race, geographic location or religious beliefs have a gene that persuades them to be kind. However, not everyone has a similar motivation to be kind; this compelling power is stronger in some than in others.

You may be wondering if 50% of happiness is in your DNA, why are you not happy all the time or at least half the times? This is explained by a genetic priority where a human being is created in a way that the genes take charge of the whole being depending on how important they are. The most basic triggers happen to be very self-centered, such as response to danger, hunger and so on, in order to help preserve life. These self-serving genes take priority leaving the other non-urgent responses to take the secondary place. For this reason, although being kind and compassionate may occur naturally, it is impossible to act on the virtues all the time. It is very easy to be caught up with life events hence allow all the other responses to overpower kindness and that is when unhappiness kicks in. This does not mean that your happy genes are lost; it only means that they lie inactively as you continue to be unhappy.

No one has control over what life throws at him or her but everyone has a say over how he or she responds to things. You get to decide how you feel and react to things and ultimately how happy or unhappy you are. However, some people may not be in complete control of how they feel or respond thanks to a gene mutation. The MAOA gene is divided into two, the happy and the warrior gene. The happy version is responsible for controlling the process of releasing dopamine, serotonin and other happy causing chemicals in the brain. It also helps retain high levels of monoamine transmitters in the brain hence boosting the person's mood. Studies have shown that this gene only causes happiness in women even though it is present in both men and women. Study shows that women who have even one copy of the MAOA gene tend to be much happier than those who do not have it. Men who have the gene, on the other hand, were reported to be as happy as those who did not. Some researchers claim that the testosterone hormone present in men cancels out its effects while others believe that the happy version in women is the same gene that is responsible for range in men.

The MAOA gene, the warrior version, is said to be responsible for the outrage and over aggressive behavior in most people especially men. This gene has been associated with uncontrollable negative behavior such as alcoholism and antisocial behavior in most men as well as a few women. The warrior gene is carried in the X chromosomes but since men have only one copy of the X chromosome, they exhibit the negative characteristics caused by the warrior gene.

Women, who have two or three copies of the X chromosomes, have free X chromosomes hence they are only carriers of the gene but do not exhibit the negative characteristics it causes. Some people who have the warrior gene tend to be extraordinarily angry.

If you do not have the 'happy' genetic combination, not to worry, happiness is also a skill that can be cultivated over time. 40 percent of your happiness is dependent on the way you adapt to deal with life situations. When you adapt effective ways, you become happier and more fulfilled. It is comforting to know that you have free given happiness that lies within you, all that is required of you is to learn how to condition it.

Human beings have the ability to adapt to situations hence they can consciously dictate the course their lives take. The choices you make affect your happiness in one way or the other and if you are careful to make more decisions whose result is positive and fewer options whose result reduces your happiness, you are definitely bound to be happier. The ability to mold your life to get a life you desire lies within you, you may, however require a bit of training to be able to take full control of your emotions. Until recently, it was believed that the human brain remains the same throughout their lives, which would mean, you would be limited in the amount of changes you can make in your brain to improve your response to events. Thanks to scientists, you will be pleased to know that this is not the case. The brain has the ability to expand to accommodate new information. The learning and molding processes do not end at childhood unless you want them to because with a bit of training, you can develop to amazing extents. Now you have no excuse to be unhappy.

There are a few things that can help you tap into the trained happiness, they include:

Changing the way you think and react to situations.

The behavior you portray and your actions can actually enlarge or contract various regions of your brain. They can either fire up circuits or calm them down. A good illustration would be if you worry too much on a regular basis, you activate certain brain pathways. Changing the way you react to situations may help reduce the anxiety hence retraining your brain to silence these pathways and build up new ones at the same time. That way you will no longer take those long rides down the worry freeway.

Choose actions that will help alter your brain's structure.

The more you utilize your brain, the more it expands to help accommodate the new tasks. It does this by either growing in size or by shrinking or reducing the space dedicated to performing tasks that are rarely performed. For example, if you usually go into a miserable mood whenever you are faced with problems, your brain is accustomed to that habit. Your brain will continue to react in a similar manner until you instruct it to come up with resourceful ways to solve your problems. If you start facing your predicaments, your brain will automatically shut down or significantly reduce the misery pathways because they will be less useful. It will also reinforce your creative pathways and you are more likely to experience more happy moments.

Use imagination to trick your brain

The brain does not have the ability to detect a lie from the reality when responding to stimulation. This is the reason why people get the 'flight or fight' even in the absence of any life threatening danger. New technology used in performing brain scans has shown that both human beings' conscious view and their imagination activate similar brain areas. Consequently, you can reduce the effect of excruciating memories by imagining a less agonizing past, which will in turn rewire the past recorded in your brain. Using mental pictures can also help train your brain to be and stay happy. The brain cannot make a distinction between a real experience and an internal fantasy. If you can constantly fill your mind with images of you being happy and take time to visualizing the desired images long enough, your brain will suppose those things happened in reality and you will be happier.

The most obvious but, unfortunately, the least momentous source of happiness is the external environment. It contributes about 10 percent of the total happiness. In fact, critics say that it is a negligible source of happiness due to its short lifespan. A great life, achievements, weather and any other external factor that makes you happy are too real to ignore. However, it only lasts for a few minutes, hours, days, or months at best and only a few seconds at worst. The feeling you get when the dealer hands you the keys to your new car, when you say 'I do' to your dream partner or when you wake up to beautiful sun rays cutting through your curtain is all too real. It is awesome and priceless, for a few hours or days after, you may still have that awesome feeling and you can confidently say you are happy. Sadly, this feeling does not drag on forever, soon enough you get used to your new status and the spark is long gone, replaced with a hunger for something new, and if possible, better. Relying on events, achievements and circumstances for happiness are like a constant chase after the wind. It is impractical to expect anything to be constant enough to guarantee your happiness and even if you find that special thing, you are likely to get used to it and it will no longer have the same effect it once did.

Chapter 3: The Myths of Happiness

Nearly everyone buys into the myths of happiness. Nothing can guarantee unending happiness or eternal misery, there are no defined rules and situations for happiness so do not agree with your mind or anyone who tells you that some people were designed or are simply meant to be happier than you are. Research shows there are no magic pills to happiness and no defined course to misery. Happiness is subjective to the individual.

Whatever situation life throws at you, good or bad, is an opportunity for growth and a chance for you to change to a better version of who you are. *Life only presents an opportunity and the decision on how to respond to them is entirely up to you.* If you believe that happiness is not for you, you are likely to manipulate the situations that come your way to misery and vice versa. This is probably why you may believe that the myths are true because you subconsciously make situations work for or against you. Here are a few popular myths surrounding the subject of happiness.

Happiness is seasonal.

Life has its ups and downs and, therefore, it is impossible to be happy all the time. This is not true. Human nature is happiness. Research shows that, in the absence of any emotions, the mind is usually in the state of mild curiosity, which is itself a positive emotion and can be associated with happiness. Negative emotions that are associated with unhappiness are not naturally occurring and they are usually triggered. You can enjoy constant happiness regardless of the things happening in your life or around you. It is possible to be broke and happy or jobless and remain happy but only if you adapt your attitude to the situation.

Most people assume that life events have a huge impact on happiness but the way you react to those events is what determines your happiness. If you can continuously find the good in every situation, including the ugliest situations, then you can enjoy happiness every day of your life. Happiness should be a constant state and not a seasonal feeling.

Happiness just happens.

Happiness is not something that will happen to you, it is rather something you create. Most people are in the hunt for the ultimate thing that will make them happy and that is mainly the chief reason behind unhappiness. Happiness is acquired when someone feels that their life is meaningful and they have a significant level of fulfilment. Such a life does not just happen; it takes hard work and a lot of determination to reach a point of self-approval. There is no single time when you will reach a point in your life when you hear a voice or see a sign indicating that it is time to be happy so if you are waiting to discover happiness, you are most likely going to be unhappy for the rest of your life.

As pointed out in earlier chapters, happiness lies within you. It is, therefore, proper to conclude that no matter what you get that lies outside of your being will never get you out of the hole of unhappiness that you feel trapped in. There is no magic recipe to being happy, you need to evaluate your life, find the cause of unhappiness and work towards eliminating it and if possible replace it with something that can make you happier. You must understand and know yourself.

Happiness is dependent on accomplishments or failures.

From views, that certain achievements such as wealth, marriage and kids will make you eternally happy to beliefs that certain failures such as divorce, health or money problems will make you unhappy for the rest of your life. "If I get a car, buy a beach house, marry the girl or the man of my dreams and have a great career, I will be happy." Have you ever caught yourself saying this? It is a lie. If you allow something, even one thing, stopping you from being happy, chances are you are never going to be as happy as you want. Sounds harsh? It is not meant to, it is just the truth. If you are honest with yourself you have had other excuses in the past and you even had similar marks as to when you will be happy. When you were 10 years old, your problem was never a beach house and a great career so your target might have been along the lines of "If I get more friends, I will be happy." Time passed and you got more friends, but you wanted more and, therefore, the statement changed to "If I become popular with the girls or boys (accordingly), I will be happy." Then it was if you got a girl/boyfriend and so many years later, you still aren't happy.

You have to reprogram your mind to view life as something without a defined meaning. *Live to enjoy life.* Achievements are great, but they are never guaranteed so, if you live with the sole intention to achieve something, you are likely to be disappointed. This is because either you might not achieve your goal and/or when you achieve it you will discover that although it will make you happy, it will not meet your expectations of providing eternal happiness. When you achieve one goal, your target shifts and you want more so you will always be on a never-ending chase. It is okay to be ambitious, but it is even better to be ambitious and happy at the same time. There will never come a time when you accomplish enough, but you can train yourself to appreciate what you have already accomplished and you will be astonished to discover just how happy you can be even as you work towards your goals. Your focus on situations can alter your happiness.

There is also a popular misconception that more of something will make one happy. If you are not content with the one car you own already, what makes you think that two, three or even ten cars can make you happy? You may be thinking that since achievements were meant to make you happy and they did not, you need to achieve more. This is not true. Some people are born to be happy.

As much as genes play a role in a person's happiness, it is improper to dismiss the power everyone has in improving how happy they can be. You are as happy as you decide or choose to be and not as happy as your genetic composition dictates. Your nature plays 50 percent role to your happiness but if you bury it in all the turmoil and chaos of this life, it is very easy to forget how to be happy. Here is a story that clearly explains how this may happen.

There once was a golden sculpture in the middle of a certain city, it was so beautiful that it made the neighbouring cities were green with envy. One day, there was news that some people had planned to steal the golden sculpture so the city dwellers decided to cover it with stones, that way the thieves will not find it. True enough the golden sculpture was safe thanks to the stone disguise. However, the city dwellers did not bare the sculpture after the raid. A few years passed and no one remembered that beneath the heap of stones lay a golden sculpture. Just like the golden sculpture, if you do not exercise your naturally existing happiness, you eventually forget that it exists within you.

Even if you do not or you suspect that you might not have the 'happy' gene, it is not the sole source of happiness. Every human being has an inner joy that is not dependent on genes or events surrounding you, all you need to do is find it. You can cultivate happiness and train your brain to be as happy as you want. Do not go blaming fate for your unhappiness; you have everything it takes to restore your happiness.

Chapter 4: How to Achieve Happiness

Your happiness is your responsibility, not just to yourself but to the world too. It is paramount that everyone learns how to be happier because, at the end of the day, that is what life is all about. Research shows that the best way to guarantee your happiness is by knowing who you are and learning to be comfortable in your skin. Most people will agree that it is easier said than done. However, it is possible and here are a few tips that will put you on the road to happiness:

Make a choice to be happy.

This may sound obvious but very few people make a conscious decision to be happy. The world is full of disappointments and chaos thus being happy does not come as naturally as many would wish. Being happy is a goal as any other that requires to be defined in details for it to be achieved. Working towards happiness is a lifelong journey, one that you need to be devoted to. You need to know what you need to be happy, how to achieve that status as well as how to maintain the happiness. All these are conscious decisions that you can only make if you *choose to be happy*.

Be around happy people.

Happiness is contagious and so is negative energy. If you spend most of your time around happy people, you are likely to acquire positivity from them. Just the same, if you spend too much of your time around grumpy and unhappy people, you will eventually become as grumpy as they are. Being around happy people will also teach you how to respond to situations positively, you can use them as your role models. Every time you find yourself in a tricky situation and you start getting negative emotions, ask yourself what a certain happy individual would do, say or think if they were in your situation and do that too.

Happy Homework

List your top five companions. Who are the top five people that you spend the most time with? More than likely, you are an average of these five people. Is this a good thing or a bad thing?

Learn to control your emotions.

For you to be happy, you need to participate fully in your life, take in the good and the bad but choose to respond positively instead of menacing over the suffering life throws your way. Evil and good things happen to both those who are happy and those who aren't. The only difference is in the attitudes these people have towards the acts of life. Most people have been through traumatic experiences and so many others, almost everyone, have regrets but the effects of the regrets on individual's happiness differ from one individual to the other. This has very little to do with the experience since the experience may be similar for some people; it, however, has a lot to do with how you choose to respond to the situations. For instance, take two people who have a past of sexual assault. If one of the two decides to take the experience as proving that they can survive anything and the other one dwells on the daunting experience. The person who takes it as an opportunity to be a stronger and better person is likely to be happier than the one who sulks about it year after year while constantly focusing on the pain.

Even the worst experiences have a positive aspect, learn to look for that good thing and capitalize on it instead of focusing on the bad all the time. This does not mean that you should ignore the bad things that may happen to you from time to time. Recognize the bad too but do not dwell on them, solve what you can and leave what you cannot. After all, brooding over them will not improve the situation, if anything it will lead to unhappiness.

Start your day positively.

Your morning can make or break you. The way you begin your day defines how your day will be and how you spend, your days define your life. For this reason, you should be very careful to design your morning for an upbeat day.

Perform activities that will help harness your positive energy. According to emotion experts, you must have at least 1:3 negative to positive energy to experience any substantial level of happiness. This means that you need three positive experiences to restore the energy of one negative experience. In today's world that is filled with so many distractions, there is no better time to strap up those positive emotions that early in the morning. Starting your day on a high note also sets a happy foundation for the entire day. Studies show that even if you may not have 100 percent stress free day, starting your day right can keep your spirits high at least until noon. You can consciously choose to start your day with momentum to feel great.

Visualizing a happy day, affirming your happiness, exercising, meditating and planning your day are some of the things that you can incorporate in your morning routine to ensure a happier life. Be sure to wake up an hour or so earlier than usual. Make your exercises regular and you will notice how happier and productive you will become.

Learn to let go.

A wise man once said "All attachments are suffering." Nothing in life is constant. People and things are always changing. If you do not adapt to such changes, you will forever be unhappy. If something does not work out as you expected it to, learn from it and move on. There is no point in holding on to things that keep hurting you. If, for instance, you are in a bad relationship, you hate your job, or you are unhappy with any aspect of your life, maybe it is a high time you call it quits instead of hanging in there hoping that things will get better. If something happened in the past that is all it is, the past. Do not let it define you or dictate the kind of life you are going to lead. You deserve to be happy so purpose that no one or nothing will stand in the way for that.

You only have one life to live so do live it in happiness. It's really your choice.

Express gratitude.

Everyone has something to be grateful for. Being grateful is something that you should do on a daily basis. Sometimes it may be hard to be grateful when you do not see any reason to be grateful. They say that as long as you are alive, you always have a reason to give thanks but sometimes, your life isn't what you want it to be. Have you even thought about the simple things? How miserable would you be if you didn't have a roof over your head? What about the clothes on our body? Could you be thankful that you can breathe clean air, walk, think, speak, live, etc.? The small things we often take for granted. Showing appreciation for your life puts you in a higher vibration. Like attracts like.

Learn to incorporate it into your behaviors for your own good. When you are ungrateful, you tend to push away the things you want in life because even though you may not spell it out, people can pick on your un-appreciation. Never postpone gratitude until something happens, for instance, you cannot say you will show gratitude when your friend or family member does something to prove to you that they care. By doing so, you will be giving away the power to choose when to be happy. You might as well say you will be happy when the other person decides to show you that they care. Bearing in mind that there are no guarantees in life, this is not a wise move. Practicing gratitude is more beneficial to you than it is to the person being appreciated. People who are thankful tend to be less resentful and happier as compared to those who aren't. It also extends your physical health and strengthens your social connections. This can also strengthen your bonds to others.

If you get in the practice of being constantly grateful, you are most likely going to be the 'glass half full' kind of a person. This coupled with showing people that you appreciate them also goes a long way to enhance your happiness. Getting into the habit of being grateful trains you how to get past anger and hurt because you have to get past the negative emotions before you can find something to be thankful for. Also comparing whatever is causing you pain, to the list of things you are grateful for may help soothe your anger. The best way to ensure that you stay grateful is by incorporating hobbies as tasks that help you keep track of the good things in your life into your daily routine. Writing a gratitude journal, get into the habit of saying five or more things that made your day to your family and have them do the same and writing gratitude letters are some of the ways to stay grateful. When you are consciously looking for things that make your day, you are more likely to be and remain happy.

Happy Homework

List 20 things in your life that you are grateful for. If you list any people be sure to let them know. Call or write a letter expressing your gratitude for them in your life. Notice how you feel during this process. This is such a powerful activity. *You will INSTANTLY start to feel happier*.

Create social connections.

Close, caring relationships are crucial to your well-being as well as happiness. Relationships form a psychological space that provides safety making it easy to exploring and learning processes. When you feel safe, you will be inclined to exploring new possibilities. Research shows that people who have a sound social life tend to be happy and they have health benefits in that they hardly contract mental illness. They also have a short illness recovery period. This can help reduce stress as well as boosting positive emotions. Being a member of a group will give you a sense of belonging.

Both introverts and extroverts benefit equally from being social. Happiness is highly contagious. Spend time with happy and positive individuals and watch your happiness increase. Remember: You are the average of your top five companions.

Engage in more laughter and smiling.

Smiling and laughing heals everything from the heart, mind, and to the body. A smile has the power to swing a negative emotion to an upbeat one so learn to smile through your good and bad experiences. When you smile, the world smiles back at you. This is very true. People who smile a lot tend to be happier and they also have better social lives because everyone prefers to be around a happy soul.

The movement of muscles to produce the 'ha ha ha ha!' sound when laughing triggers a raise in the concentration levels of endorphins, popularly known as the feel good feeling. Study also shows that laughter is one of the highest contributors to bonding. When a group of people share things that make them laugh, they not only lift each other's spirits but also they tend to develop and maintain strong bonds amongst themselves.

Happy Homework

Find a way to work comedy into your life. Watch a funny movie with friends. Learn a funny joke to share with others. Look for opportunities to laugh with people and notice the connection it creates.

Create goals and ambitions.

Setting goals and achieving them is one of the most satisfying things in life. A number of studies support the theory that people who have set goals and are committed to achieving them are happier than those who do things aimlessly. This may be because when setting goals, you show a great deal of self-confidence, consciously or subconsciously. You only set goals as high as you think you are capable of reaching. Having goals to work towards gives you a sense of purpose, this goes a long way in reducing negativity. Further studies show that people get more satisfaction from achieving goals that are challenging to achieve. This may have something to do with the fact that most goals are usually of less value. Be careful not to set unrealistic goals as they could have an unwelcome opposite effect. If your goals are unachievable, it can be very frustrating and make you feel unhappy. If you want to be truly happy, do not sell yourself short though.

Perform acts of kindness and helping others.

When you are kind to people, you not only feel proud of yourself but people tend to like you more. These two factors are imperative in boosting your spirits hence making you happier. Genuine caring is what I'm talking about. People can easily spot fake kindness. Even when you feel like you have nothing to give back to the world, consider the saying 'when you help heal other people's wounds, your wounds heal faster.' Therefore, going through difficult situations is not a valid excuse as to why you don't extend kindness or lend a helping hand to someone in need. If anything, it should be the reason why you do kind deeds. The ripple effect on kindness is infinite. Who knows how just a smile can affect the entire world?

Use the power of now.

It is surprising that the people with little material possessions tend to be happier than those who are wealthy. The question is, why? This is because the wealthy spend most of their time multiplying their riches, which has very little influence on happiness, while the middle class people spend most of their time building relationships and savoring their experiences. Living in the present and watching as life unfolds is one of the most powerful contributors to happiness. Learn to appreciate that the present is all you have and the only time you have control over. It is impossible to ignore either your past or your dreams for the future.

Dwelling on the things that already happened or spending all your time daydreaming about your future, knowing very well that you cannot live in either place is time wasting and can be depressing too. Living in the present will help you embrace fulfilling experiences that you would have otherwise overlooked. Day dreaming can make you have unrealistic expectations, which could prevent you from being happy. For instance, if you have an image of your dream spouse stuck to your mind, the one who always says and does what you consider the Mr./Mrs. 'perfect ,' you are more likely to find flaws in anyone who doesn't fall under your 'perfect' category. Very rarely do things turn out as perfect as you picture them in your mind. You can never get long lasting state of happiness by daydreaming of what you want to have in the future or by wishing that you had made different decisions in the past. The past will always be there so the best thing you can do is learn from your past, prepare for the future and most importantly, live now because it is all you have. Each moment you can make decisions to create a better future and past.

Create an exercise routine.

You may be familiar with the term 'runner's high' also known as endorphin rush. This is the feeling that one gets during and after working out session. When you work out, your levels of feel-good neurochemicals such as serotonin, norepinephrine and dopamine in your body are boosted. In addition, exercise raises the levels of brain-derived neurotropic factor abbreviated as BDNF, a substance that protects the brain from emotional disarrays as well as repairs the brain cells damaged by excessive stress and depression. Lastly, it enhances the release of hormones that are very similar to opium, endocannabinoids and endorphins, which flood your system making you feel relaxed and at peace.

Exercising at least once a day, 3-4 days a week is highly recommended but working out twice a day, especially in the morning and evening, will be more beneficial as you will be happier, focused and more productive. Whenever you are agitated or you are feeling overwhelmed, working out can help calm your nerves down. Another thing that works for most people is incorporating fun in the workout. Exercising can be hard work, but it doesn't have to be. Working out with a friend, having your favorite music playing as you work out or if your workout includes activities such as running, gorging or bike riding, you can opt to work out outdoors instead of going to the gym. Pay attention to the small things such as lovely weather, the kids playing and not forgetting to take a route with beautiful sceneries so that you can appreciate nature as you work out.

Chapter 5: How to Experience Happiness for Longer

Very few things are more depressing than finding something you have been looking for only to have it slip between your figures. If you don't want to find out first hand just how depressing losing your new found happiness can be, here are some tips for you.

Maintaining happiness is just as important as finding it is. It is also a tricky task because the feeling of contentment is very elusive due to human being's curious nature. When you find something that makes you happy, say a brand new car or a new hobby that keeps you excited, you are likely to stay happy for a relatively long period. With time, the feeling of contentment and joy is replaced with the weight of the additional responsibilities that come with the 'feel good' thing. In the place of material possessions such as a car or a house, you start thinking of how to service it. If you have acquired new social or formal status and you feel happier, the challenge would be how to maintain your newfound status. You also get used to the new thing and although you may still experience positive emotions, they reduce over time and in some cases, they diminish. Your mind starts to hunt for a new and more exciting experience.

The satisfaction treadmill is also to blame for your short-lived happiness. Once you achieve your goal, your target automatically shifts. For instance, if you have been working out and eating healthy to be a size 10, achieving it will not make you content forever. After celebrating your great results for some time, you will want to lose more weight. Consequently, the happiness brought about by the initial weight loss is no longer enough to sustain positive emotions. Luckily, there is a way you can prolong the happiness period to ensure that you stay happier for longer. The techniques that help with this adaptation are appreciation and variety.

Variety
This is the most basic and probably the most efficient spice of life known to mankind. It advocates for constant change so that people do not get too familiar with things that bring about happiness. When your experiences are always new and unforeseen, you are less likely to get used to them to the extent of getting bored. The quick turn of events means that you always have something to be excited about. However, this technique fight against adaptation and it is not always practical. In addition, if an event or experience is repeated many times, you can easily predict the outcome hence you do not get the same thrill out of it.

Study shows that if positive changes are experienced in dissimilar ways, they tend to result to longer lasting happiness. Doing things differently can help you get the thrill of a new experience. For instance, if you do different things with your spouse, you are likely to have a more satisfying and happier marriage life. You will also love your job if you have new challenges to tackle everyday instead of having a daily routine that you stick to day-after -day. You are likely to love your home more if you change the decor regularly. Mixing things up will help reduce the rate at which the excitement fades. This technique will only help prolong the happiness derived from an experience, but do not expect it to last forever.

Appreciation
To appreciate is defined as the act of paying attention or notice to someone or something. When you appreciate your

positive experiences, you allow your mind to drift back to them repeatedly in joy and amazement. This not only extends the period you remain happy for but it also goes a long way in boosting your self-confidence. People spend a lot of time trying to figure out what will make them happy, but not enough time trying to hang on to the happiness they have. In a way, all your energy on making more money, without any thought this focus to what you want to do with the money you have already earned. The key to wealth, as the key to happiness, is not only to look for new opportunities, but to make the most of the ones you already have at your disposal.

Final Thoughts

This book does not offer you a quick fix for your misery dilemma or promise you a magic pill that will instantly make you a happier person. This is because there is no such thing as a shortcut to happiness. Happiness is and has always been something that one needs to work towards every day of their lives. It is quite a shame that most people have thrown away the authentic meaning of true happiness. Some have even replaced it with a generation 'X' definition, which portrays happiness as a manufactured state of mind. Unless people change this mentality, misery and depression related illnesses will continue to ail the world.

True happiness comes from within. If you look inwards, realize the things that make you happy, and focus on capitalizing on them. For instance, if your strong points are kindness, find a way to incorporate kindness in your day-to-day activities. Happiness is not a destination but a lifelong journey. Only those who commit to cultivate it tirelessly get to reap the sweet fruits of constant happiness. You may not try all the tips that you have read in this book but make sure you choose a few that suits you best and apply them consistently. You will not find happiness instantly so you will need to be patient and committed in order to get positive results.

A Note From the Author

I wish you the best on your journey through life. I wrote this book to share my ideas and personal experiences about happiness with you. I hope that you were able to find some points and ideas to implement into your life to make it better and happier. Just remember that happiness is what you make of it. Enjoy the wonderful things in life and appreciate the beauty of it all. Be happy today!

Cheers,

Noah Shelton

Made in United States
Troutdale, OR
08/19/2023

12189389R20029